Soap Making Recipes Book 5: Lard Soap Recipes

By

Angela Pierce

Table of Contents

Introduction 5

1. Lard Soap Recipe 11

2. Olive and Lard Soap Recipe 13

3. Fast Lard Soap Recipe 15

4. Creamy Lard Soap Recipe.. 17

5. Alternative Lard Soap Recipe 20

6. Honey and Oatmeal Lard Soap 23

7. Crystal Lard Soap Recipe 26

8. Laundry Lard Soap Recipe 29

Thank You Page... 32

Soap Making Recipes Book 5: Lard Soap Recipes

By Angela Pierce

© Copyright 2014 Angela Pierce

Reproduction or translation of any part of this work beyond that permitted by section 107 or 108 of the 1976 United States Copyright Act without permission of the copyright owner is unlawful. Requests for permission or further information should be addressed to the author.

This publication is designed to provide accurate and authoritative information in regard to the subject matter covered. This work is sold with the understanding that the publisher is not engaged in rendering legal, accounting, or other professional services. If legal advice or other expert assistance is required, the services of a competent professional person should be sought.

First Published, 2014

Printed in the United States of America

Introduction

The health and beauty are most concern issues of today's busy world. No matter how much we spend in terms of time and money, it won't be effective unless we choose rightly. Only the right medicine can heal you same goes for beauty, if you do not choose the right things for your daily hygiene and beauty regime, the achievement of desirable effects will always remain a dream. The thing we utilized every day for cleaning and beautify our skin is soap. It is the only thing you never fail to use daily.

So it means your 70% beauty is totally dependent on the soap you utilize and the ingredients it contains. If you are not using the right soap for your face, it means you are effecting your 70% of the beauty. Can you take that much risk for your skin? Obviously not, then why not to wisely choose the right soap for your skin. Don't be frightened that this will take time, because figuring out the right soap among a lot of brands available in the market, it's quite time consuming and most of the time we end up falling back to previously chosen one. Apparently, it seems a lengthy process but thanks to a homemade soap process as it has totally customized the soaps according to our choice and skin type.

Yes, it is true. Now you can prepare your own soap at home with all natural and hygienic ingredients carefully catered at your clean and healthy kitchen. Isn't it great? But wait the great news is that you are totally free to use any ingredient of your choice and quite easily. When the natural beauty is possible and so easy then why wasting your time on chemically made soaps. The homemade soaps are not only healthier, but also provide you more natural and pure beauty without causing any damage to skin which otherwise caused by harsh chemicals commonly utilized in the soaps available in the market.

Making soap at home will not only save you a lot of time and money, but also provide complete charge over your beauty regime. You can even customized your soap with not only the ingredients of your choice but also adding beautiful colors, fragrances and contours. It's like your beauty soap is totally dependent upon your mood or choice. You can not only prepare beauty soaps at home for your own self and family, but also can customized it according to the choice of your friends and gift them on their birthday, Christmas and any other special occasion. Moreover, if you are a creative geek then believe me to fulfil your craving for innovation and creation, making soap at home is the fantastic idea. So why not start making soap at home and amaze your family and friends with your another creative art. This is the time to do something new and beneficial at home, even you can engage your spouse and kids in this creative time.

This is also a good business opportunity for you, if you are a house wife or a creative being and looking for something to start with. Homemade soaps have caught a lot of attention of women to adopt as a new business idea. It's not just a perfect way to utilize your creative abilities but also your time. The best thing is, it will also earn you a good amount of money and a lot of appreciation for your creativity. A good self-satisfying and accomplishing art, then why to give this business a second thought? Get some wonderful recipes to start with and add your creative charm in them by customizing soaps with your favorite ingredients and fragrances.

Although there is a lot of ingredients to choose from, but when it comes to get the best for your skin, then the things which must be taken care is that your soap must be enough moisturizing to provide good protection against harsh weather especially in winter. Most of the people prefer to use lard in the soaps to make their soaps more nourishing, protective and moisturizing. The best thing is it is easily achievable ingredient and you can even get it free from any market or shop. So why not to take benefit of this wonderful ingredients which comes with a lot of benefits like:

1. Lard is the ingredient which you can easily get from any nearby butcher shop in reasonable charges and even sometimes free.

2. By using lard you can save some healthy ingredient to be wasted away in the dustbin and protect nature balance and utilize it in a more productive way.

3. Lard prepared soap last longer and provide you with thick leathery baths.

4. It is enough moisturizing to keep your skin protected from dry and harsh weather.

5. It provides enough hardness to soaps to last them longer in running water.

6. It will provide your soap with good base and smoother look.

7. You can not only utilize lard in beauty soaps, but in your laundry soaps too.

8. It's a good way to invest your time in some creative and productive activity like soap making and keep trying in mixing out some amazing ingredient together to get your next amazing soap for your new business.

9. Making Soaps at home will save you a lot of money and most importantly a good protection for your skin too.

10. You can easily get these soaps by making at home at less than the cost you buy them from market and with no natural ingredients but just chemicals.

Making soaps at home has a lot of benefits and in quite recent years, it has been greatly encouraged too, because of the bad chemical effects and expensive cost. You can even make laundry soaps by using lard.

Here are some awesome recipes not only for preparing beauty soaps, but for laundry too.

1. Lard Soap Recipe

Ingredients:

-12 to 16 oz of water (Distilled)

- 32 oz of Lard

- ½ ounces of fragrance oil (any of your choice, but preferably rose fragrance)

- 4.25 oz of Lye (100% sodium hydroxide)

Instructions:

Take all ingredients and measure them carefully. Melt the fat completely and add in it the essential oil. Mix the lye in the water and heat them up. Now add in the lye solution the melted oil solution. Now combine both the solutions well and stir well. Take the mold and pour this solution in the molds and let them cool down. It will take 4 – 5 hours or more. Once the soap solution gets hardened like a soap unmold it and cut it into desirable shape. For more hardened soap keeps the molded soap for some weeks to dry out completely. This recipe will give you beautiful soap bar for your beauty regime, but if you want this soap to be colored then you can use any color of our choice while preparing soap solution.

2. Olive and Lard Soap Recipe

Ingredients:

-76 grams of Sodium hydroxide (Lye)

- 30 grams of Castor Oil

- 36 grams of essential oil (any of your choice)

- 300 grams of Lard

- 228 grams of Water (Distilled)

- 270 grams of Olive oil

Instructions to Prepare:

First of all carefully measure all the ingredients. Measure lye and essential oils and set aside to start preparing the soap. Now take a water in a bowl and carefully add in it the lye. Make sure you do it in a well-ventilated room and never add water into lye but always lye chunk by chunk into the water. Dissolve the lye into the solution until it's clear completely.

Take all the essential oil, fat and butter in a pan and heat them on low heat till melted down well. Wait for oil to cool down a little bit. Now add the oils into the lye solutions and stir both mixtures well until they made a good smooth mixture together. You can use wooden spatula for making mixing more easy. While mixing be careful as mixture is quite hot and it can be splashed over your skin and clothes. Once the mixing process has done, add in it the colorants and fragrance oil and again stir it well.

Now take a mold of any shape and design, carefully pour in it the mixture until fill. Now place the mold in a cold place to let your soap hardened and dry out. It will take some hours at least 5 – 6 hours for proper hardening. Once the soap gets hardened, unmold it and cut it into bars if necessary. Now your soap is ready to use but if you want to store them for later use then it's quite easy, as you can wrap them in a plastic wrapper and keep them in s safe place. You can even gift them to your loved ones by wrapping them into a gift paper or putting them elegantly in a gift basket. A great way to present someone on Easter especially to kids.

3. Fast Lard Soap Recipe

Ingredients:

-228 Grams of Water (Distilled)

- 20 grams of fragrance oil

- 600 grams of Lard

- 80 Grams of Lye

Instructions:

Take the distilled water in a bowl and add in it the lye carefully. Stir this mixture well until clear. Be careful never add water into lye as it could be dangerous because activated lye is harmful. While dealing with it, be sure about your safety by putting your goggles and gloves on. It is better if you dress yourself into a full sleeve shirt to avoid any injury.

Take the lard and essential oil in another pan and heat them on low flame until melt down. Now wait for some time until the temperature of the oil gets down. Now mix the lye solution and oil mixture together gently and slowly until a smooth look of a mixture is achieved. Now you can add any colorant or dye if you want, otherwise the original white color of the soap is also not bad.

Take a mold and pour in it the soap mixture carefully. Now set aside the mold for 4- 5 hours for the soap mixture to cool down and get hardened. Once it's done, unmold the soap and use the amazing fragrance and healthy homemade soap. It is the basic and instant recipe following which you can prepare soap in less time. If you want to give a different look and color to the soap, then you can do it by adding ingredients of your choice.

4. Creamy Lard Soap Recipe

Ingredients:

- 120 grams of wheat germ oil

- 60 grams of avocado oil

- 228 grams of distilled water

- 120 grams of palm kernel oil

- 36 grams of fragrance oil or essential oil of your choice

- 60 grams of cocoa butter

- 240 grams of Lard

Direction to Prepare:

Before proceeding towards the soap making process, it is essential to put on your goggles, full sleeve clothes and gloves to be safe from any injury.

Take all the ingredients and measure them carefully one by one and put them in the proper place or in bowls. Clean the place well where you are intending to make soap. Choose an ample free time to prepare soap and keep your kids and pet out of the place to avoid any distraction and mishap.

Now take a bowl and pour into it the distilled water. Add in it the carefully weighed lye chunk by chunk and stir the solution well until it's clear. Lye is a vigorous reactor so never add water into it, but always remember that you have to add lye into the water.

Take the fat and essential oil and all other oils in a pan and heat them all together on a low flame until melt and combine together. Remove the pan from flame and wait for the mixture to cool down a bit. Now add the lye solution in the oils and mix both the solutions together until a thick smooth mixture is achieved. You can use a wooden stick for mixing as it is little tricky work and should be done quickly. But do not splash the hot mixture on yourself so carefully treats it.

Once the mixing process is done, add the additive and fragrance oil in it and stir well. Now take your mold and pour in it the mixture. Cover the mold with the plastic cover and let it cool down for 5- 6 hours in a cold and airy place. Once the soap is completely cool down and hardened, unmold it and cut it into any shape if required. You can immediately use your soap, but if you want your soap bars to run longer under the tap, then its best to place the soap bars in the wreck or shelf which is quite airy to dry out for 2 – 3 weeks. Here you go a creamy leathery soap with full of fragrance and beautiful colors in ready to use. This lard soap is quite moisturizing and do not cause dryness and roughness like other soaps. You can gift them these wonderful soaps to your loved ones.

5. Alternative Lard Soap Recipe

Ingredients:

-36 grams of Essential oil or Fragrance oil (you can choose any of your favorite ones)

- 150 grams of coconut oil

- 228 grams of water

- 390 grams of Lard

- 86 grams of sodium hydroxide

- 60 grams of cocoa butter

Directions:

Take out all your ingredients and weigh them carefully using any standard measuring instrument and you can buy them by weighing at the shop. Clean up the place where you are intending to prepare the soap as it will ensure complete hygienic environment to prepare healthier soap for you and your family.

The next important thing is to take care of protective measure like putting up full sleeve clothes, gloves and goggles to avoid any injury as you are dealing with vigorous content like lye.

Now take the bowl and add in it the distilled water which you have already measured carefully, now add in it slowly and gradually lye and keep on stirring the solution until it turns into a clear solution. Take another pan and put it on the heat at low flame. Add in it the lard and oils to let them melt down. It will take some minutes. Once all the oils are completely melted down and combined, remove the pan from the flame and let it cool down to attain a normal temperature.

Now mix lye and oils together and start stirring the both mixtures until combined well. It takes little bit of your efforts to combine them together, but be careful do not splash the mixture over your skin and clothes as it is still hot and can cause burning. Once the mixture get mixed well and turn into a smooth thick mixture, add in it the fragrance oil and any colorant of your choice. Stir it again till combine well.

Take the mold and pour in it the soap mixture and cover it with the plastic cover. Place the mold in a cold environment to dry out, it will take 5 or 6 hours. After it unmold the soap and if necessary cut it into bars.

Now place these bars on shelf where environment is enough airy. Let them placed on the shelf for 3- 4 weeks to get hardened completely. Now your soap is ready to use and you can even gift them to your family and friends. The contents are customizable and you can add any content in it to make it more suitable for your skin type and even can play around with color and design of the soap to make it more appealing to you and your family.

6. Honey and Oatmeal Lard Soap

Ingredients:

- 12 oz of goat milk

- 18 oz of water

- ¼ cup of honey

- 4 oz of canola oil

- 11.35 oz of lye

- 20 oz of coconut oil

- ¾ cup of oats (grounded)

- 40 oz of lard

- 2 oz of honey, oatmeal and milk fragrance oil

- 16 oz of olive oil

Directions to prepare:

Take all the ingredients and weight them properly. Put them in bowls and containers to be instantly available when required. Clean the place before starting to cook your soap mixture. Take on your gloves, full sleeve clothes and goggles to protect yourself from any injury as we are going to make our soap through hot process.

Take the distilled water already weigh in a container or a bowl. Add in it gradually and slowly the lye by stirring alongside. Be careful, never add water into lye as lye could be dangerous when activated so always add lye into the water. Now stir the solution well until clear. Take a pan, add in it all the oils, fat and lard except fragrance oil and place the pan at heat on low flame until all the fat get melted. Now remove it from the heat and let it cool down a little bit. Once the oil's temperature gets down add in it the lye mixture and stir the both mixtures together until make a smooth and thick mixture.

For quick and flawless mixing use a wooden spatula otherwise you can use your regular spoon too though it will take little more effort and time. Once the mixture in combined well, add in it the fragrance oil and any colorant of your desire. Stir the mixture again.

Take the soap mold and grease it with oil, pour the soap mixture in it slowly and gradually until filled. Now cover it with a plastic wrapper and put it at cool and ventilated place to dry out completely for 5- 6 hours.

Unmold the soap and cut it into bars, you can still feel the bar is quite soft and will not survive for long at running water. So, if you want to enjoy your homemade soap for long then its best to sow some more patience by putting them in an airy place to dry out completely for at least 3 -4 weeks.

Once the soap is get hardened completely, it is ready to be used or you can wrap your extra soap bars in the plastic and place them in safer place for future use. It could be a good gift to present on special occasions to your family and friends by wrapping these soaps in glittering paper or gift papers. Even you can place them in baskets alongside with candies to give your kids a healthier, safe gift for their better future. This recipe will provide you with a moisturizing soap which will keep your skin clear, white and healthy as it has all natural ingredients and hygienically prepared with your own safe hands. Enjoy this amazing fragrant soap and let others appreciate your creativity.

7. Crystal Lard Soap Recipe

Ingredients:

-16 oz of Lard

- 0.4 oz of fragrance oil

- 6.4 oz of olive oil

- 12 oz of water (distilled)

- 8 oz of coconut oil

- 1.6 oz of canola oil

- 4.54 oz of lye

Instructions:

Take all the ingredients and carefully weigh them by any measuring instrument, put them in separate bowls and containers. Do not mix up any ingredient before, so keep them separate. Clean the place well to ensure complete hygienic environment for the soap preparation. Be careful of your safety and put on full sleeve clothes, gloves and goggles to avoid any injury. Keep your pets and kids away from the room to avoid any mishap and distraction during soap preparation.

First of all take the distilled water and carefully add in it the lye chunk by chunk. Stir this mixture until it gets clear and all the lye gets dissolved. Now take a pan and put it on the heat at low flame. Add in it all the fat, lard and oils except fragrance oil and let them melt down for some minutes. Once the oils get melted completely, remove the pan from the flame and let it for some minutes until its temperature gets down a bit. Now add in it the lye mixture carefully. Mix the both mixtures together, you can even use wooden spatula for smooth mixing but any other spoon will also work but with little bit more effort and time. Stir the mixture until it attains a smooth and thick paste like shape.

Now add in it the fragrance oil and mix it again. Take a soap mold and grease it with a little oil to prevent sticking of soap mixture to the pan. Pour into it the soap mixture and cover it with the plastic wrapper. Place the mold in a cold place for 4 -5 hours. Unmold the soap and cut it into the bars. Now you can use your soap, but if you want your soap to last longer than its best to show some patience by putting your soap in an airy place for 3 -4 weeks to dry out completely. The soap will get hardened and will last longer under running water. You can wrap your soap bars in a plastic to keep them safe for future use and even you can gift them to your family and friends.

8. Laundry Lard Soap Recipe

Ingredients:

-2 oz of fragrance or essential oil (Optional)

- 8.4 oz of lye

- 20 oz of water

- 4 lb of lard

Instructions to Prepare:

All ingredients must be weighed properly and carefully. Set a suitable time to prepare soap which lead to least distractions like other work, pets, kids etc. The place must be clean and hygienic. Protect yourself by wearing gloves, goggles and full sleeve shirt. The process won't take long if you have all the ingredients weighed and well arranged in different bows and container to use instantly.

So start by preparing a mixture of lye and water, for it take the water in the container and add in it the lye chunk by chunk. Stir the solution well until it gets clear. Now place a pan on low flame and add in it all the oils and fat like lard except the essential oil. Let them melt down completely for 5 – 6 minutes. Remove the pan from the heat and let the oils to cool down till 110 degrees. Once cooled, add in the lye mixture and mix both the mixtures together. Use some easy mixing spoon or wooden spatula to attain a smooth thick mixture.

Once the both mixtures get combined well, add in it the fragrance or essential oil of your choice (it's optional). Stir or mix the mixture again. Now take the mold, you can take any kind of mold, as its laundry soap and will be grated to be utilized so shape does not matter a lot. Pour the soap mixture into the mold and cover it with the plastic cover to protect it from dust and other particles. Now place the mold in a cool airy place to dry out for 6- 7 hours. Once the soap gets dry, unmold it and you can grate it and utilize it straight forward. But if you want to use later on wrap the soap in a plastic wrapper and place on the shelf for later use. Your own laundry soap is ready to use. You can add charming fragrances in the laundry soap too, which will scent your clothes with beautiful fragrances and make you feel more fresh and active.

By making soap at home will provide you with a lot of freedom in choosing ingredients especially the color and fragrance. You can even give your clothes refreshing scent by adding some cool fragrance oil in your laundry soap. By following above methods you can not only make beauty soaps, but also laundry soaps. These soaps contain pure natural ingredients which are quite protective for your skin and especially for kid's smooth and sensitive skin. Wrap these soaps in beautiful covers to present someone or decorate your bathroom with pretty looking and smelling soaps, now it's all in your hands.

Thank You Page

I want to personally thank you for reading my book. I hope you found information in this book useful and I would be very grateful if you could leave your honest review about this book. I certainly want to thank you in advance for doing this.

www.ingramcontent.com/pod-product-compliance
Lightning Source LLC
LaVergne TN
LVHW021745060526
838200LV00052B/3489